BANDITO THE PUPPITO
DREAMS OF A HOME

BANDITO EL PERRITO SUEÑA CON UN HOGAR

100% of profits donated to help dogs in need

Illustrated by
Marcela Ramirez

Interpreted by
Reneé M. Jaime

Written by
Natalie Pate

For all the dogs I've been lucky enough to love.

Thank you, Henry Hughes, for your feedback and encouragement; Marcela Ramirez for your beautiful illustrations; Reneé Jaime for your thoughtful interpretations; Dancing Moon Press for supporting a first-time author; my pack and my family (chosen and given, human and furry) for your unwavering love and support.

Bandito the Puppito
copyright © 2020 Natalie Pate
First Edition

All rights reserved. No part of this publication may be reproduced, stored in, or introduced into a retrieval system, or transmitted in any form, or by any means (electronic, mechanical, photocopying, recording, or otherwise) without prior written permission of the author, except in the case of brief quotations or sample images embedded in critical articles or reviews.

Hardback ISBN: 978-1-945587-39-9
Paperback ISBN: 978-1-945587-40-5
Library of Congress: 2020903962
Natalie Pate
Bandito the Puppito
1. Dogs; 2. Animal Shelters; 3. Pet Rescue; 4. Pit Bull
Book Design: Dancing Moon Press
Cover Art & Design: Marcela Ramirez
Translation: Reneé Jaime
Author photo: Danielle Peterson Photography

Dancing Moon Press
Bend, Oregon USA
dancingmoonpress.com

In dog shelters, there are all kinds of dogs.

En los albergues, hay toda clase de perros.

There are big dogs and small dogs.
Short dogs and tall dogs.

Hay perros grandes y perros pequeños.
Perros bajitos y perros altos.

There are fluffy pups. And jumpy pups.
And roly-poly, lumpy pups.

Hay perros esponjados y perros asustadizos.
Y llenos de grumos y gordinflones.

There are dogs who love to sleep. And dogs who love to eat.
Dogs who like to run. And dogs who chase your feet.

Hay perros que les encanta dormir. Y perros que les encanta comer.
Perros que les encanta correr. Y perros que persiguen tus pies.

Some are shy. Some are bold.
Some are young. Some are old.

Algunos son penosos y otros son intrépidos.
Algunos son jóvenes. Otros son viejitos.

But in one special shelter was one special dog.
Bandito the Puppito, he was lovingly called.

Pero en un albergue especial había un perro especial.
Bandito el perrito, le llamaban con cariño.

He wore a mask on his face and smiled without fail.
He had spots like a cow from his nose to his tail.

El usaba una máscara en su cara y sonreía sin falta.
Él tenía manchas como una vaca desde su nariz hasta su cola.

And every night when he went to sleep:
The noise of the shelter and cold underneath:

Y cada noche cuando él se iba a dormir:
Con el ruido del albergue y el frio bajo el piso:

He'd close his eyes tight and snuggle his feet,
And dream of the family he wanted to meet.

El cerraba fuertemente sus ojos y acurrucaba sus patas,
Y soñaba con la familia que él quería conocer.

Bandito dreamed of his people, so loving and kind,
Who would come home each day to have a fun time.

Bandito soñaba a estas personas, amorosas y buenas,
Quienes venían a la casa diariamente a pasar un tiempo de diversión.

Bowls full of food, and treats, mountains tall,
They'd rub his belly; play fetch with his ball.

Con platos llenos de comida y golosinas del tamaño de una montaña,
Ellos le sobarían la panza y jugarían a ir por la pelota.

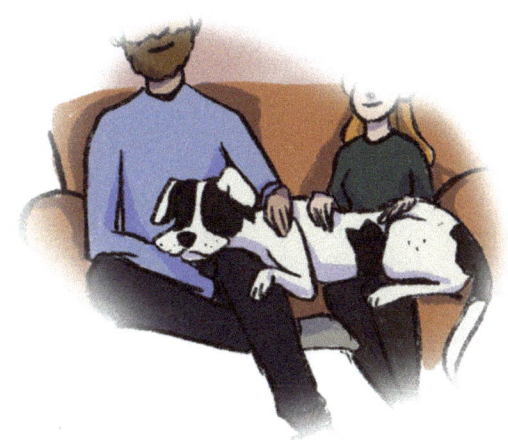

They'd take walks outside, then cuddle and rest.
They'd tug with his toys and make quite a mess.

Ellos daban paseos afuera, después se abrazaban y descansaban.
Ellos tironeaban con sus juguetes y hacían un gran lío.

But the best time of day was when they climbed into bed.
They gave him a kiss, and that's when they said:

Pero la mejor parte del día sería cuando se subían a la cama.
Ellos le daban un beso y es cuando le decían:

"We love you, our Bandito. What more can we say?
We love you even more than we did yesterday."

"Nuestro Bandito, te amamos. ¿Qué más podemos decirte?
Te queremos aún más que ayer."

When Bandito awoke in his flat shelter bed,
He stood up to stretch and scratched at his head.

Cuando Bandito despertó en su cama plana en el albergue,
Se levantó a estirarse y se rascó la cabeza.

He looked at the others and he started to sigh.
He wished his dream had come true overnight.

El vio a los otros y comenzó a suspirar.
A él le hubiera gustado que su sueño se hiciera realidad durante la noche.

"But, why not today?" he'd think to himself.
"Maybe, today, I'll go home somewhere else."

"¿Pero, porque hoy no?" Pensaba para el mismo.
"Pude ser que hoy, iré a casa en otro lugar."

So, he sat and waited for his family to come,
As he watched each friend leave, one after one.

Entonces, él se sentó y esperó el regreso de su familia,
Mientras que el veía a sus amigos irse, uno tras de otro.

But one day was different, one day was new.
Bandito could tell that his family was due.

Pero un día fue diferente, un nuevo día.
Bandito podía saber que su familia estaba por llegar.

In walked a woman with hair red as the sun.
She had freckles galore and seemed pretty fun.

Entró una mujer con el cabello rojo como el sol.
Ella tenía pecas en abundancia y parecía divertida.

Bandito perked up his head and stood up to see.
He thought to himself, "She has spots just like me!"

Bandito espabiló su cabeza y se levantó para ver.
Se dijo a sí mismo, "¡Ella tiene manchas igual que yo!"

She sat on the floor and rubbed at his ears,
She smiled so wide, and her eyes filled with tears.

Ella se sentó en el piso y le sobó las orejas,
Ella sonrió con una amplia sonrisa y sus ojos se llenaron de lágrimas.

"This is the one," she said to the man,
Who was standing above, a treat in his hand.

"Este es el único," ella le dijo al hombre,
Que estaba de pie, con una golosina en la mano.

The man bent down and snuggled in close.
"You know what? You're right. I love him most."

El hombre se incline y lo abrazo de cerca.
"¿Sabes que? Tienes razón. Lo quiero más que a los demás."

They gathered his toys, his leash and his bowl.
Then walked to the car and made their way home.

Ellos juntaron sus juguetes, la correa y su plato.
Caminaron al auto y se fueron a casa.

At first things were strange, it wasn't quite right.
But homes, as they say, aren't made overnight.

Al principio las cosas fueron extrañas, aun no estaban bien.
Pero los hogares, como dicen, no se hacen durante una noche.

Bandito's family made sure he was cozy.
They gave him so many kisses, his cheeks turned rosy.

La familia de Bandito se aseguró que él estaba cómodo.
Le dieron tantos besos, que sus cachetes se sonrosaron.

They gave him a bath, which he didn't quite like.
But after, he ran 'round like a super-speed bike!

Lo bañaron, lo cual no le gustó mucho que digamos.
¡Pero después el corrió en círculos como una bicicleta a súper velocidad!

They took him for walks and loved to explore.
And after every adventure, he'd always want more.

Lo llevaron a caminatas y disfrutaron explorando.
Y después de cada aventura, él siempre quería más.

Day by day, things started to seem,
Little by little, more like his dream.

Al paso de los días, las cosas comenzaron a verse,
Poco a poco, más como sus sueños.

Bandito knew he was safe, he knew he was loved.
He knew every day would be more and more fun.

Bandito sabía que él estaba seguro, él sabía que lo amaban.
Él sabía diariamente que sería más y más divertido.

But the best time of day, he knew from the start,
Was when they settled in bed and opened their hearts:

Pero la mejor parte del día, él sabía desde el principio,
Fue cuando ellos se acomodaban en la cama y abrían sus corazones:

"We love you, our Bandito. What more can we say?
We love you even more than we did yesterday."

"Te queremos nuestro Bandito. ¿Que más te podemos decir?
Te queremos aún más de lo que te queríamos ayer."

The Real-Life Bandito

Natalie Pate and Josh Gwin adopted Bandit in October 2016. They found him thanks to Savin' Juice, a nonprofit dog rescue in Oregon that specifically helps dogs with severe medical needs. Though Bandit did not have health problems, he spent the first two years of his life in shelters. When the rescue found him, he was living in a shelter with a high euthanasia rate, especially for pit bull type dogs like Bandit. Bandit now spends his days lounging in his rocking chair or playing neighborhood watch from the upstairs window. He gets two walks and countless treats every day. When his family comes home, he runs to his bed, plants his face and sticks his booty in the air to get the best scratches. He goes on frequent road trips and outdoor adventures. His evenings are filled with playtime and cuddles (he especially loves to dissect the squeakers from stuffed animals). He's mastered the art of giving kisses when someone is upset. And every night, he sleeps under the covers between Momma and Papa.

About the Author

Natalie Pate is a Colorado-born, Oregon-based journalist. When she isn't writing (or cuddling Bandit), she's probably off dancing, singing, finding new places to explore or spending time with her friends and family. Natalie volunteers weekly as a reader for the nonprofit SMART Reading, a one-on-one mentorship program that helps children cultivate a love of reading and provides them free books for their own collections. She also volunteers with Fences for Fido, a nonprofit that builds fences for families with dogs tethered outside for long periods of time. She has her family and fiancé, Josh, to thank for her deep love of animals. Being able to share Bandit's story while helping other dogs has been her dream since she first saw Bandit's adoption photo and said, "I just have a feeling about him." She and Josh hope to open their own rescue one day.

How Your Purchase Helps

Bandit's adoption wouldn't have been possible without the constant work of animal rescues, shelters and foster networks. To thank them, 100% of the book's profits will be donated to further dog rescue and adoption efforts. Learn more at banditothepuppito.com.

Follow Bandit and Share Your Story

You can follow Bandit's real-life adventures by checking out @BanditoThePuppito on Facebook and Instagram, @BanditoPuppito on Twitter. Share your own rescue story using the hashtag #BanditoDreams.

www.ingramcontent.com/pod-product-compliance
Lightning Source LLC
Chambersburg PA
CBHW051355110526
44592CB00024B/2992